D0462243

THE GOOD NEWS

FROM GOD

A Fresh Perspective on

Christianity, The Bible, Church and Life

This book is a gift to you from

_____

TABLE OF CONTENTS

Introduction

1. Everlasting Life 9

2. The Bible 13

3. In the Beginning 19

4. After the Fall 23

5. Jesus 31

6. Salvation 37

7. Grace and Mercy 45

8. After Baptism 49

9. Church 51

10. The Blessing 59

P.S. A Touching Letter (from a new brother in Christ) 61

Introduction

There are two groups of people for whom this book was written—those who are looking for answers to basic questions about the Bible, Christianity, church and the abundant life, and those who already have those answers, but are looking for, perhaps, a better way to share that knowledge with others.

The first group is made up of people who are ready to learn: some who now have small children at home and feel a need for direction, and a change in lifestyle, to properly raise those children; some who have experienced one or more difficult, life-changing events, such as a divorce, the loss of a job, radical health issues or the death of a loved one; and it has awakened them to the need to find God. For whatever reason, they are just ready to make a change and are seeking guidance.

The second group is made up of good-hearted Christian people who want to share the gospel, but are uncomfortable doing so. It may be that, though they understand the Bible well enough for themselves, they feel inadequate in their ability to teach others.

They may be hesitant to intrude into someone's life for fear that they may cause offense. They don't want to be pests and create a rift in personal or professional relationships, but would like to share God's good message with those who are lost.

This book was created to fill a need by putting all the key information into one, easy-to-follow, easy-to-understand and easy-to-share format.

With this book, the person seeking a better way will not only find clear, concise answers to his questions about how it all fits together, but will receive guidance on the best way to move forward after receiving that basic information.

With this book, the more knowledgeable believer will no longer have to worry about what to say. By making this book avail-able to others, perhaps by just leaving it on a table or giving it as a gift, the seed will automatically make its way to the good soil that has been prepared to receive it—without creating offense.

So, whether you are someone who is ready to learn about Godly things for the first time, or a knowledgeable Christian looking for an effective way to share the good news, this book is for you.   May it bless your life abun-dantly.

1

Everlasting Life

What may well be the most quoted scripture in the Bible says, *For God so loved the world, that he gave his only begotten Son, that whosoever believeth in him should not perish, but have everlasting life* (John 3:16).

"Everlasting life!" We like the sound of that—especially when we consider that it will take place in heaven where there will be no sorrow or pain. "No more suffering." That sounds very appealing.

In the end, our goal as Christians is to have that everlasting life and to help as many other people as we can to have it too. But our goal is not *just* about "in the end."

It is also about "in the mean time," and "right now." Jesus addressed that as well. He told us in John's gospel that he *came that we may have life, and that we may have it abundantly* (John 10:10).

He was talking about having the abundant life now; a life of joy and peace and love, in spite of the problems we face on a daily basis; not just after we pass on to the next level.

So how does one sign up for this abundant life and the everlasting life to follow? Before we get to that, we need to lay a little ground work. Hopefully we can put it in a way that will make it clear.

First, let's look at a few things about the
Bible, because it is through this wonderful book that we can learn the answers to
so many questions, including those about
life and getting to heaven.

2

The Bible

Putting it plainly, the Bible is the inspired word of God. This means that, ultimately, God is the author, though he did use the pens of men to write it.

Though the Bible looks like one big book, it is actually a collection of sixty-six smaller books pulled together into one collection. These books contain a variety of styles, or genres. They generally fall into categories like history, prophecy, poetry, wisdom, literature or letters (called "epistles" in some Bibles), just to name a few.

The Bible was written over a period of about 1500 years in three different languages (Hebrew, Greek and Aramaic). It was written on three different continents (Africa, Asia and Europe) by about forty different authors.

As you can imagine, these authors came from a variety of backgrounds. There were shepherds, kings, prophets, fishermen, doctors, and others. Most of them never knew one another personally.

This collection of books share a common storyline about the creation of the heavens and the earth, as well as man, the falling away from God by man, and the redemption and restoration of man back to God.

They also share a common theme, about God's deep love for all of humanity; and a common message, about salvation—being saved from the eternal penalty for sins. The message is that this salvation is available to all who repent of, which means "to turn away from," their sins and commit to following God with all of their heart.

In addition to sharing these commonalities, these sixty-six books do not contain any historical errors or contradictions.

God's word truly is an amazing collection of writings. Can you imagine trying to put sixty-six different books together that were written over a 1500 year time period by so many people from so many backgrounds and having them all fit together without error or contradiction?

It certainly is a masterpiece. It is the work and the word of the *true* master, God.

Two Main Sections

The Bible is divided into two main sections. The first section, called the "Old Testament," is made up of thirty-nine books. These books deal with God's relationship to man before the coming of Jesus.

The second section, the "New Testament," is made up of twenty-seven books and begins with "the gospels" (which means "the good news") including **Matthew, Mark, Luke** and **John**. These tell about Jesus' life here on earth, from birth to death, and then his resurrection (being raised from the dead) and ascension (going back into heaven).

After that comes the book of **Acts**. It tells us about the establishment of the church here on earth. This is where you will find the most examples of baptisms.

Next comes the largest group of books, twenty-one in all, sometimes called **"the epistles."** These were actually letters written to the various churches, or individuals in the churches, to help them better understand how to serve God and how to treat one another in a Godly way.

The final book is called **The Revelation**. It talks about the end times and heaven.

As Christians, we study the scriptures, sometimes daily, to try to better understand how God, our creator, wants us, the created, to live. We know that he loves us and wants the very best for us. And it is here, in "the word," that we seek his answers to guide us.

Now, let's get back to the life and salvation issues—according to the Bible.

Note: A portion of the description of the Bible in the first half of this chapter was derived from an article found at http://www.christianministriesintl.org/articles/Bible-the-Inspired-Word-of-God.php. Used with permission.

3

In the Beginning

In the beginning, God created the heavens and the earth. He also created man, starting with Adam and Eve. You can read all about this in the book of Genesis, the first book in the Bible.

At first, God's relationship with Adam and Eve was perfect, because they trusted him totally and they obeyed him in every way.

He placed them in the Garden of Eden, which was awesome! It was full of all kinds of beautiful trees that were loaded with delicious fruit. Adam's only job in the Garden was to tend it and keep it.

God gave him, and Eve, a lot of freedom, and only one restriction. They were not allowed to eat the fruit from one special tree in the middle of the garden—the tree of knowledge of good and evil.

Satan (the devil) didn't really like this happy arrangement between God and man. From early on he made it his mission to destroy that relationship. When he tempted Eve to eat of the forbidden fruit, she gave in and even convinced Adam to go along with her.

As a result, God's relationship with man changed. A rift, caused by disobedience, had occurred.

As a consequence, God put Adam and Eve out of the garden and would not let them return. This not only meant that their living quarters had dropped off a notch, but it also meant that they could no longer eat of that other tree that God had also placed in the garden—the tree of life. From that time forward, their days would be numbered.

God also caused Adam (and mankind in general) to have to work hard in the fields to feed himself and his family. From that point on, thorns and thistles sprang forth from the ground, adding to the difficulties man would experience.

God also made it so that childbearing would be very painful for Eve and the mothers to follow.

The harmony was gone. There was separation from God. There was pain and suffering. It was, truly, "Paradise Lost."

But God's love for Adam and Eve was still there. It did not change. And he loved their descendents. He longed to restore the broken relationship between himself and man. He longed to restore eternal life to his earthly children.

But being totally just (as in "justice"), he couldn't do that without someone having to pay the price for their sins.

Over time, Adam and Eve and their descendents populated the earth. You can read about a lot of these descendents in the first two books of the Bible, Genesis and Exodus.

4

After the Fall

Abraham

Though there were several key figures in those early days, one of the main ones was a man named Abraham. He was very special because of his faith. He trusted God greatly in spite of very difficult situations.

Because of his great faith, God promised to Abraham that his descendants would be as numerous as the stars in the heavens and that, through his seed, all the nations of the earth would be blessed.

Though Abraham didn't know it at the time, the seed by which all the nations of the earth were going to be blessed was Jesus.

Abraham and his wife Sarah were childless for most of a hundred years. They eventually had a son, Isaac, who later had two sons of his own, Esau and Jacob.

Jacob (and his son, Joseph)

Jacob, whose name God eventually changed to Israel, had twelve sons. One of his youngest sons, Joseph, was his favorite, which made the brothers jealous.

When they had the chance, the brothers sold Joseph to some slave traders who were passing through on their way to Egypt.

After a series of events in which he was elevated to a position of leadership and power, Joseph predicted, with God's guidance, that there would soon be seven years of plentiful harvests followed by seven years of severe famine.

As a result of this information, Pharaoh (the king) put Joseph in charge of building barns and storing up the grain during the good years to prepare for the hard times that would follow. Then, when the famine arrived, Pharaoh put Joseph in charge of distributing the grain to the people.

The Egyptians were not the only ones who had experienced the famine. People from neighboring lands did as well. When Joseph's father, Jacob, heard of the availability of grain in Egypt, he sent his sons to buy some for his large and growing clan (family).

When the brothers got to Egypt and saw

Joseph, they did not recognize him as their brother. Joseph did recognize them, however, but he harbored no bitterness toward them. He understood that it had all happened for God's good purpose.

Joseph eventually revealed himself to his brothers and was soon joyfully reunited with his father. Since the famine was far from over, Joseph convinced his father to move the whole clan to Egypt where their needs could be met.

After Joseph and the brothers had passed away, the descendents of Jacob, these "children of Israel," grew very numerous. In fact there were hundreds of thousands of them, or more.

This rapidly growing population began to worry the Egyptian rulers. Out of fear of being overrun by these children of Israel, the Egyptians decided to enslave them to keep them under control.

So, the Israelites became slaves and remained that way for four hundred years. When the Egyptians became very oppressive, the children of Israel cried out to God for help. He heard their cry and responded by sending Moses to tell Pharaoh to "Let my people go!"

Pharaoh did not want to let them go at first, but finally agreed to after God sent ten plagues onto the Egyptian people. Pharoah changed his mind, however, after they had been released, and sent his army to bring them back.

To help his children out, God parted the Red Sea so they could cross over on dry land to the other side. When the Egyptian army followed, God let the water return to its normal state and the Egyptian soldiers all drowned.

You can read all about this incredible event in the book of Exodus.

10 Commandments

It was while these liberated children of Israel were wandering around in the desert that God gave to Moses the stone tablets upon which he had written the Ten Commandments.

God also told Moses about many other laws, memorial feasts, sacrifices and rituals that the children of Israel were to obey and to perform during this time.

However, they did not always obey the laws perfectly—they were, after all, people just as we are! Offering sacrifices was the way that God had instructed them to seek his forgiveness, though the sacrifice of animals was not able to take away their sins.

These children of Israel in their tribes were eventually given their own land on which to settle. This became the Kingdom of Israel. Some years later there was a major split in the family.

The Kingdom of Judah

The ten northern tribes split off from the two southern tribes, (made up of) Judah and Benjamin.* This southern union became known as the Kingdom of Judah. It was in this kingdom that the city of Jerusalem was located. It was also from this Kingdom of Judah, the "Jews," that Jesus eventually descended.

Through the years God's people basically abandoned him and began worshiping foreign gods and idols. Therefore he allowed the Babylonians to carry them off into captivity and to destroy the Temple.

Another of the tribes, the tribe of Levi, whose people were known as the Levites, did not receive its own land because its tribesmen were the priests who offered the sacrifices for all of the people. To do that, they were necessarily scattered throughout all of the other tribes. In time, these very religious people became most associated with and present in the kingdom of Judah.

After seventy years in Babylon, some of the Jews were allowed to return to the Holy Land—to Jerusalem, to the rebuilding of the Temple and the city—with a renewed appreciation for obedience.

As a result, they no longer worshipped foreign gods and idols, but adhered strictly to the Law, intent on the mindset of not getting it wrong. Over time they became fanatical rule-keepers.

In fact they became so strict in their rule-keeping that they began missing the whole point. Their lack of understanding caused them to eventually clash—even with Jesus, God's own son.

5

Jesus

When the time was right, Jesus was born of a virgin, Mary. The Holy Spirit, who is also God, was his true father. So, in reality, Jesus was the son of God and, at the same time, the son of "man."

Though he amazed the biblical scholars with his knowledge and understanding when he was only twelve years old, Jesus didn't officially begin his ministry until he reached the age of thirty. That's when he began the quest to once again reconcile, that is to restore, the relationship of man to God.

Even though the Old Testament had prophesied of a savior, a messiah, who was to come, the religious leaders of Jesus' day refused to recognize the fact that Jesus was that messiah.

They viewed him as a troublemaker who was continually challenging and disrupting their long-held religious beliefs. In their eyes he was a disruptive force that needed to be stopped—at all costs.

In one way their view of him was right. He *was* a troublemaker for those who were more interested in keeping a set of religious rules and regulations than in showing love to God and to their fellow man.

He *was* a troublemaker for anyone who was more into feeling superior and self-righteous and in lording it over people than in encouraging, comforting and making a positive difference in their lives.

Jesus' life—His message—was so radically different from anything that had ever been lived or taught that he changed the world.

Instead of teaching "an eye for an eye, and a tooth for a tooth" he taught, *If someone strikes you on the right cheek, turn to him the other also* (Matthew 5:39).

Instead of teaching, "Love your neighbor and hate your enemy," he taught, *Love your enemies and pray for those who persecute you* (Matthew 5:44).

Instead of parading his righteousness in front of people, Jesus taught, *He who wants to become great among you must be your servant* (Matthew 20:26).

He believed and taught what has come to be known as the golden rule, that is, *Do unto others as you would have them do unto you* (Matthew 7:12).

Jesus was humble and taught his disciples to be humble. He taught them to not show favorites but to treat poor people with just as much respect and love as they did the rich people (James 2:3).

He was willing to serve others and taught his disciples to *not think more highly of themselves than they ought,* but to *consider others better than themselves* (Romans 12:3; Philippians 2:3).

Jesus never practiced his religion with an attitude of trying to impress others about how righteous he was. His whole purpose was to seek and save the lost and to bring glory and honor to his father in heaven (Matthew 6:1; Luke 19:10; John 14:13).

Jesus came and showed, by his life and

teachings, that God wants more from someone than just a willingness to keep a set of rules. He wants our hearts. He wants our love—for him and for our fellow man. Only then can we live a fulfilling life.

Eventually, as also had been prophesied, when he was thirty-three years old, the religious people of his day crucified him—they nailed him to a cross. To make sure he was dead, they pierced his side with a spear. He bled while hanging on the cross.

Just think about that. They, the most religious people of his day, the ones who were supposedly looking for the messiah—they were the ones who wound up crucifying him.

It just goes to show that just because someone is religious doesn't mean that he or she is Godly or right. Never forget that. It's still true today.

After his death, Jesus was wrapped in burial clothes and laid in the tomb. But the story didn't end there. Three days later Jesus rose from the dead. He then appeared to his disciples and to more than five hundred people.

Then, after the forty days, Jesus ascended back into heaven to prepare a place for those who would believe in him.

6

Salvation

Before going back into heaven, Jesus spoke with his apostles. These were men he had specially selected to carry on his work after his ascension back into heaven. He instructed them to go to Jerusalem and wait.

It was while they were there that the Holy Spirit came upon them and gave them power to do miracles and to speak

in languages they had never studied and
to preach the word about Jesus and his
church.

It was during this momentous occasion
that Peter, one of the apostles, told the
crowd about everything that had just
happened and about how this Jesus, who
was actually the son of God, was the one
they had just crucified.

The Bible tells us what happened next. It
says that Peter told the crowd,

*"Therefore let all Israel be assured of this:
God has made this Jesus, whom you crucified,
both Lord and Christ."*
*When the people heard this, they were cut
to the heart and said to Peter and the other
apostles, "Brothers, what shall we do?"*
*Peter replied, "Repent and be baptized,
every one of you, in the name of Jesus Christ
for the forgiveness of your sins. And you will
receive the gift of the Holy Spirit. The promise
is for you and your children and for all who*

are far off—for all whom the Lord our God will call."

With many other words he warned them; and he pleaded with them, "Save yourselves from this corrupt generation." Those who accepted his message were baptized, and about three thousand were added to their number that day (Acts 2:36-41).

The Beginning of the Church

This was actually the beginning of the church, when God added these three thousand people into his book of life.

And, in the bigger scope of things, this is when man was reconciled (made right) with God.

Though not one of us who is alive today was there when Eve and Adam were separated from God, and though none of us were physically there when Jesus was crucified, the truth is that when we sin today, we are just as guilty of causing our own separation from God as they were back then.

The Bible confirms that we are all sinners, every one of us. But the Bible also confirms that every one of us can be reconciled, restored back to God, as well. We can do this by becoming Christians—children of God.

How to Become a Christian

To do so we must truly believe and confess that Jesus is the Christ, the son of God (Romans 10:9-10); we must repent of, which means to turn away from, our sins, and be baptized in the name of the Father, Son and Holy Spirit for the remission (forgiveness) of our sins. At that point we will receive the gift of the Holy Spirit and God adds us to his church (Acts 2:38-41). It's that simple. It's that basic.

When to Become a Christian

Some people hesitate to become Christians because they feel like they don't know enough about what the Bible teaches. They think they need to wait until they know a lot of scripture first.

But the truth is that most baptisms in the Bible took place after very little teaching—usually after one sermon. And the Bible refers to new Christians as *newborn babes* and tells them to *desire the sincere milk of the word, that ye may grow thereby* (1 Peter 2:2).

Just as with newborn babies, most of the learning and growing takes place after the birth/baptism, not before. You just need to know and believe the very basic principles about Jesus as stated in the paragraphs above.

Some people hesitate to become Christians because they don't feel like they are good enough yet. They want to wait until they've got their life under better control before they take that giant step.

These are noble thoughts, but they miss the point. The truth is that you will never be good enough—no matter how hard you try. You will be waiting for the impossible, because you can never, ever, in a million years, be good enough, on your own, to deserve to be saved or to go to heaven. It can happen only by God's grace.

The whole point is that Jesus loved you so much that he was willing to come and to die in your place. When you believe, repent, confess and are baptized, your sins become his sins and his purity becomes your purity.

Your baptism—going down into the water and being raised up again—is an expression of faith which symbolizes the death to your old *evil* self, the burial of your old *evil* self, and the resurrection of your new, *pure* self.

You are made clean by the blood of Jesus and from that day forward his blood/sacrifice continually washes away your sins.

We talked about God's grace a moment ago. A little more needs to be said about that and about God's mercy, as well. They are both very important.

7

Grace and Mercy

Grace

Grace means "unmerited favor." It means that God gives us a gift (of eternal life) that we don't deserve and that we cannot earn. It is a free gift that he gives to those who *choose* to believe in him.

Since we can't earn it and since it is a gift from God, we must always and continually give the glory to God for saving us.

It's not that he needs the glory or the praise. *He's God!* It's that, as our creator, he knows that our most fulfilling, peaceful, loving, abundant life can be lived only if we are humble and grateful to him for our blessings.

If we are so arrogant because of how great we are personally, we undermine the things that would bring us true joy.

Mercy

The other side of that grace coin is mercy. Grace means we get something we *don't* deserve, and mercy means that God does not give us what we *do* deserve—eternal punishment and separation from Him.

When Jesus died for us, he took on our sins and in fact became sin for us. He took on what he did not deserve, so we wouldn't have to. And when he was raised from the dead, he overcame the devil for good. He became victorious forever.

We now have been given the opportunity to join him in that victory if we will just believe in him, confess his name, repent of our sins, be buried with him in baptism and be raised again in newness of life.

Included in that "we" is "you." You have been given the opportunity to be a child of God. Don't pass up this great blessing.

He really did die for you. And he really does love you—just as you are. Accept his grace and mercy and become a new creature in him.

If you are ready and willing to take this important step, contact someone to make it happen. Don't put it off. It's too important.

8

After Baptism

Then what? What happens after baptism? That's a good question! We're glad you asked.

As newborn babes, we need nurturing. We need family. We need love. All of those things are necessary to help us to continually grow into mature, spiritually-minded children of God. And that is a lifelong process.

And it is next to impossible to do it without assembling with other Christians who are farther down the road of Christian maturity than we or any new Christian would be. We need nurturers. And that's where "church" comes into play.

9

Church

The word "church" roughly means the assembled, those called out for a specific purpose. It's used in the broadest sense in that there is really only one church— the one that the Lord adds you to when you are baptized.

In a more specific sense, we also use the word "church" to talk about a smaller group of believers, a congregation of disciples, who meet in a local place to encourage one another and to study about God and how to live the Christian life.

People sometimes use the word "church" to designate a building, but that's not really the church. That's a "church building." The real church is the people, the disciples, the Christians.

Finding the "Right Church"

As a new Christian, it is so important to find a Godly church—a church with the right heart and spirit. There are a couple of things to keep in mind in that regard.

First, remember what we talked about before. Just because someone is religious doesn't mean he or she is right. This will always be a fact of life. Keep it in mind.

Second, just as there are dysfunctional families raising babies to be dysfunctional adults, there are dysfunctional "spiritual" church families raising their "spiritual" babies to be dysfunctional as well. Avoid these families at all costs.

Instead, find a spiritually healthy church—one that is loving and caring and causes you to want to be more like Christ every week; one that recharges your batteries, not drains them.

This is not to say that you will find a church with zero problems. There are positive and negative things about every group of people. And there are wonderful loving people in most churches. So look for the church that most nurtures you, fills your needs and helps you grow.

So how do you find that Godly church? Let's look in the Bible for the answer.

Love

The Bible says, *By this all men will know that you are my disciples, if you love one another (John 13:35).* In another place Jesus said that the greatest commandment is to *love the Lord your God with all your heart and with all your soul and with all your mind. And the second is like it: Love your neighbor as yourself* (Matthew 22:37-40). Based on these verses, the first thing to look for in a church is the believers' love for God and for one another (including you).

If they seem distant and unfriendly, or if they seem condescending and controlling, you are definitely in the wrong place. If you don't see and feel the love, keep looking.

Bible Study

Another key to watch for is how much church members study and rely on God's word, the Bible, in determining what they believe. There is much talk in some churches about "The Bible says this" or "The Good Book says that," but they don't ever really show you where it really does say *this* or *that*.

Be firm in asking, "Where does the Bible

say that? Show me." And make sure it "smells right" when they give you an answer. If they start backtracking or giving funny answers, it may be a sign that they don't really look to God's word for the truth. You might need to keep looking.

Prayer

A third key is to pray fervently for God to show you the way. Prayer is just you talking to God—thanking him for all he has done and asking him for guidance.

Ask him to help you find a church that is pleasing to him. Ask him to guide you and to help you grow personally. Ask him for wisdom. He loves it when you ask for wisdom. He has promised to grant that request (James 1:5).

Holy Spirit

Fourth, listen to the Spirit. Remember what Peter said when the first Christians were baptized? He told them (and us) that they would receive the gift of the Holy Spirit. That is to say, the Holy Spirit would be given to them (and us) as a gift.

The Holy Spirit will be with you, to guide you and comfort you. If you are in a church and it just doesn't feel right, it may be that the Spirit is telling you that this is not the right place.

The right church will not make your stomach tie up in knots. The right church will inspire you to seek God's will and to make a difference in the lives around you. If you don't experience that uplift and encouragement, keep looking. You haven't found the right place yet.

In time, with persistence and prayer, you will find the right situation. And you will know that you are "home."

Find a Mentor

We would also encourage you to find a mentor—someone you trust and respect for the example he or she sets. Pick someone you admire, someone who is loving and kind and is continually striving to grow in the nurture and admonition of the Lord. If you can't think of someone, consider the person who gave you this book, or at least someone he or she would recommend.

Modern Technology

You may want to consider using modern technology to facilitate your growth. With the internet, it's easy to stay in touch with believers around the world.

Though there is no substitute for a wonderful group of Christians meeting together, the opportunity to study and learn and get feedback from others online can be a great blessing if used wisely.

And, there are a great many study resources on the web as well. It's something to consider.

Make a Difference

Finally, go out and make a difference in the lives around you. You don't have to wait to start making a difference. Some of the most effective spreaders of the gospel are those who have just recently experienced the joy of having their sins washed away. If you don't know what to say, just hand out this book.

Don't hesitate! Share the good news of Jesus Christ with others. Then work toward becoming a mentor to those who are not as far down the road as you. It will be one of the most rewarding and growing experiences of your life.

And always, always, always, give the glory to God. May God bless you abundantly as you strive to do his will.

10

The Blessing

We hope this book has been a blessing to your life. We would love to get your feedback and/or suggestions to help us make it even better. Our contact information is listed in the back of the book.

We would also like to pray for you, *by name*, if the book's message has touched your life. If you have become a Christian, and are now one of our brothers or sisters in Christ, please let us know so we can lift your name in prayer to our father in heaven. It would give us great joy to give thanks to God for making you a part of his, and our, family.

If your faith has been renewed, refreshed or re-energized by this message of hope, please let us know about that as well, so that we can offer a prayer of rejoicing and thanksgiving with you and for you.

If you have a story to tell, please share it with us. We will be so blessed. If you have a question about something that we've written, or need to contact us for any reason, just let us know and we will be happy to respond.

P.S.
A touching letter from a
new brother in Christ

Note: My friend, Emma, has a son, Randy, who lives in North Carolina. When she went to visit him, last year, she took a copy of THE GOOD NEWS FROM GOD and laid it on Randy's coffee table. Randy's friend, (who is a very shy person and asked that we not use his name) saw it, read it and eventually sent me his story via Emma's cell phone (he slowly hand pecked the entire letter on her phone). It was sent as one large paragraph. I've broken it up a little to make it easier to read. You may read it below :

"Mr. Dennis I heard you needed to hear my story I've been friends with Randy for a long time. MisEmma was like a Second mama to me. She kept us in line when she lived here. When She left I found myself in a lot of trouble. After one of the hurricanes. Some people convince me to steal their staffs they collect on the insurance. When they got Caught For insurance fraud They said it was all my idea They said they knew nothing about the whole plan So I went to jail for four years.

I did my time I spent a lot of time thinking. I wondered how I got myself into this mess the jail room kept get-

ting smaller and smaller. In the time longer and longer. I didn't blame anyone but myself the trouble I got into. When I got out of jail not many of my friends Would talk to me. Randy still let me come over and visit.

It was in June's mama came to visit. There was a book laying on his coffee table. I picked that up and come through it. It was real easy and simple even for me. I felt the piece come over me. I managed to read the whole thing in about two hours And I don't read real fast. The next morning when I was working on the water The The sun was Rightor the world was prettier.

In my heart I knew that God was talking to me I knew that I was important to him I knew that Jesus had died for my sins. I knew that my time but I did was nothing. Jesus had forgiven me. I knew I was totally clean That not only did God chair he loved me. I Smiled More that day than I ever did. And then I wanted to share that joy. Then you sent some more books to Randy's house.

My brothers was in jail and I sent him a copy. My best Friends Alex and Jimmy were in jail and I sent them a copy. Alex and Jimmy got saved I'm still working on my brother. Every day I wake up and I get on the water and I see The sunshine I feel like it's God shining directly on me. I never felt so important in my whole life. That God would send his precious son died for me.

You see I'm not just an ordinary guy. I'm even less than that. A simple fishermen who screwed up. I never read the Bible before It was too long and too hard to understand. And I didn't feel it was meant for guy like me. But I am real grateful for the book you sent. It's a little weather around the edges. It's made its way through a lot of people. I believe they helped a lot of them.

I know it's God that saves us But it sure was nice to have a book That made it simple. A lot of us sinners have enjoyed that book. We have benefited from it Been saved by it and if you even baptized because of it.

Ms. Emma said it was really important to you for you to hear from me I'm sorry it took me this long. I don't write To we'll   But you do need to know what impact this book had. It made its way through jails and friends. It made my life easier and Alex and Jimmy's as well. We know we're important now. And that God loves us.

Thank you and your church for sitting down and writing it so we can read it. Thank you for making it so we could understand it. I hope lots more people get to read it and understand how important they are to.

My life is so much richer because I know that God loves me. I'm excited to get my brother to that point to. I got baptized in the East River. It's where I fish every day. It made a real important to me. Again thank you to you and your church For sending out those books.

Thank you for making it simple so I could understand what God wanted me to hear. Forever in your debt.
A simple fisherman From Down East North Carolina."

How awesome is that? Praise God! May we continue to rejoice in his blessings as we gladly share THE GOOD NEWS FROM GOD!

Help us spread the good news!

The last instruction Jesus gave to his followers was, *Therefore go and make disciples of all nations, baptizing them in the name of the Father and of the Son and of the Holy Spirit, and teaching them to obey everything I have commanded you. And surely I am with you always, to the very end of the age* (Matthew 28:19-20).

This charge has been called "the great commission" and we take it very seriously. In fact, this little book, as well as the Spanish version of it, "Las Buenas Nuevas de Dios," is a response to that call. (It is also available in Chinese, French, Italian, Arabic and German (with other languages in the works.)

We would like to invite you to join with us in our efforts of making this book available to your friends, family, business associates, customers and church family.

Free Books

To help facilitate the distribution of these life changing books, we are making them available to you, **free of charge**, as long as we have funds available. Don't be shy in ordering what you need to help you spread the good news in your area.

To order your free copies, contact us at

<u>outreachchurch@outlook.com</u>

or mail your request to
Outreach church
P. O. Box 52
Hamilton TX 76531

To download the free e-book version of

THE GOOD NEWS FROM GOD
in many languages
or to learn more about its history go to:

www.goodnewsfromgodbook.wordpress.com

**Contact us for a
Free Bible Correspondence Course and/or online
Bible study resources.**

Note: Scripture references are from the King James, English Standard and New International Versions of the Bible.

Note: FYI, These books can be viewed and/or purchased at Amazon.com in paperback (though at a much higher price) as well as in the Kindle edition. (Search under "Dennis Ensor" for best results.) We would prefer to get them to you for free (since we can get them at a much cheaper price), but wanted to let you know about the availability of this other option.

TO DO LIST
(Four critical things to be done right now)

- Bookmark (or "add to favorites"), on my computer, the GOOD NEWS website address:
www.goodnewsfromgodbook.wordpress.com

- Add "Outreach church" to my address book so I can order more books when I need them:
P.O. Box 52, Hamilton TX 76531
outreachchurch@outlook.com

- Order more copies of THE GOOD NEWS FROM GOD so that I can reach out to the lost souls around me.

- Pass this copy of THE GOOD NEWS FROM GOD on to someone else while I'm waiting for my new shipment of books to arrive.

Additional good things to consider

- Write a brief note to whoever gave me this book and to Outreach church telling them how this book impacted me and how I am using it to impact those around me.

- Make a donation to Outreach church to help keep the GOOD NEWS book ministry growing so more can be reached.

- Pray prayers of thanksgiving for this ministry and for God's direction in reaching the lost.

~~~~~~

This book was given to you as part of a joint
effort between Outreach church and

~~~~~~